HOW TO PAINT
FLOWERS
& PLANTS
IN WATERCOLOUR

JANET WHITTLE

HOW TO PAINT
FLOWERS
& PLANTS
IN WATERCOLOUR

Janet Whittle

SEARCH PRESS

Dedication

To my grandchildren Soli and Gaia, you are a complete joy. Also to my husband Barry, my support system for forty-six years.

Acknowledgements

I would like to thank, in alphabetical order, Caroline, for her words of wisdom; Hazel, for sharing and caring; Linda, for telling me I could write a book and how; Lindsay, for her support and encouragement, and Maureen for guidance when the direction wasn't clear.
I would also like to thank all my colleagues and students past and present for their company and humour, and for making my working life as an artist so rich and rewarding.
Special thanks to Edward Ralph for being so good-humoured and easy to work with, and to the team at Search Press for their encouragement and calm understanding.

Originally published in Great Britain 2003 as *Painting Flowers & Plants*

Search Press Limited
Wellwood, North Farm Road,
Tunbridge Wells, Kent TN2 3DR

Text copyright © Janet Whittle 2017

Photographs by Charlotte de la Bédoyère, Search Press Studios, except for those on pages 2, 17, 21, 23, 24, 30, 31, 32, 45 (top, right and bottom), 54 and 126–127, by David Marsden.

Photographs and design copyright © Search Press Ltd. 2017

ISBN 978-178221-418-2

The Publishers and author can accept no responsibility for any consequences arising from the information, advice or instructions given in this publication.

Suppliers
If you have difficulty in obtaining any of the materials and equipment mentioned in this book, please visit the Search Press website for details of suppliers: www.searchpress.com

Publishers' note
All the step-by-step photographs in this book feature the author, Janet Whittle, demonstrating how to paint flowers and plants in watercolour. No models have been used.

Printed in Malaysia by Times Offset (M) Sdn. Bhd.

Cover:

Rhododendron 'Susan'

70 x 53cm (27½ x 20¾in)
A delicate and beautiful flower, especially in shadow. In memory of my sister whom I miss every day.

Page 1:

'Duchess of Marlborough'

51 x 33cm (20 x 13in)
This complex peony grows in a friend's garden, and I saw it in full bloom when conditions were absolutely perfect, just after the rain, with the sun shining.

Pages 2–3:

Bowl of Beauty

93 x 74cm (36½ x 29in)
The centre of the peony flower is exquisite. Here it is the subject of a painting in its own right.

Opposite:

Peony Alba Plena

51 x 33cm (20 x 13in)
I saw these *Alba plena* in a garden in France. I could not stop to paint them at the time, so I took lots of reference photographs and used them to paint a simple composition which I felt suited the complexity of the flower.

CONTENTS

Irises

51 x 33cm (20 x 13in)

These irises do not flower for very long, so you have to watch the weather and take care not to miss the best of them.

INTRODUCTION

Painting is like a journey which never brings you to a final destination. There is always something you have not yet painted, or a different colour or medium to try. The possible variations are endless, which is why I find it so exciting: it has kept me enthralled for many years.

Throughout my painting career, flowers have been one of my main inspirations. I never fail to be enchanted by the variety of colours and shapes, and the sheer perfection as the bud slowly unfolds to reveal the flower. As a painter, I have the freedom to portray them as I wish, using my imagination to change or combine colours and background tones.

I find the effects of sunlight and shadow magical. They can add an extra dimension to any painting, bringing out the colours, form and depth. I believe that it is only when you paint that you learn to observe closely enough to discover the significance of different light effects.

Every flower or plant is unique, and will respond to different techniques in different ways. Work through the exercises and practise any techniques you have not yet tried. Experiment with different approaches.

I have included some of my favourite techniques in this book. I hope you will find them useful and that, above all, you will enjoy trying them. It would take more than one lifetime to carry out every one on every flower, but I hope it will help you on your journey to improve your paintings.

Janet.

JANET WHITTLE

MATERIALS

It is not necessary to collect all the items on these pages before you begin to paint: start with a few and add more as you go along. Starting out can be expensive: generally, the better the materials you buy, the longer they will last, and the easier it will be to master painting in the way you want. After all, you would not buy sandals if you wanted to take up jogging!

The essentials, obviously, are paper, brushes and paint. The colours and paper I use now are not necessarily the ones I shall be using next year. I am always trying to improve my painting and know I always will be. It is part of the excitement that keeps me painting, and I hope it will be the same for you.

A selection of watercolour papers

▬ Paper

They say a workman is only as good as his tools, and this is a good rule to follow when choosing paper. Do not buy job lots of cheap paper, or something left over from school, or bits of unidentifiable paper that you have had given to you or have found in a drawer.

Different papers have very different properties, and it is important to understand what your paper will or will not do as this will dictate the techniques you use for a painting. The most obvious distinction is the smoothness or roughness of the paper, which will affect the appearance of your painting. Some papers will take masking fluid, but it will lift the surface of others when you try to remove it. It is more difficult to work wet-in-wet with the more absorbent papers.

I have indicated the paper I have used for each demonstration. This is the one I enjoy working with, but it may not be the case for you. It pays to experiment, and it is also fun! I use 300gsm (140lb) or 640gsm (300lb) Not. If you use the lighter-weight paper it should be stretched on a drawing board about 20cm (4in) larger than the size of the paper. Do not forget you will lose at least 2.5cm (1in) all round underneath the tape. For composition sketches, I use ordinary cartridge paper.

▬ Pencils

I use HB pencils for initial line drawings as they do not need to be too heavy. To draw in extra flowers after the initial washes, I use a 3B pencil, as this shows up over the colour and will not dent the paper like a harder pencil. For darks, or for transferring carbon to the back of a tracing, I use a 9B pencil.

▬ Scalpel

I use a scalpel or a penknife to sharpen lead pencils. For pure graphite pencils, I use a rotary pencil sharpener.

━ Paints ━

I use a variety of different makes and colours of paint, but I always choose artists' quality. These are brighter and soften easily, and though they are more expensive the effect is well worth it. Buy just a few colours to begin with, rather than starting with dozens of tubes or pans. This will help you to get to know the colour mixes well.

I am continually discovering new colours and mixes; it is part of the joy of painting. I fill up empty pans with paint straight from the tube.

A selection of watercolour brushes.

Brushes

My collection of materials includes a mixture of brushes made from both natural and man-made fibre. I have no particular preference, though I like a firm brush and synthetic fibre does tend to be firmer as well as less expensive.

When painting flowers, you will need Nos. 4, 6, and 8 round brushes for general painting along with a small (No. 00) round brush for details such as veining on petals and leaves.

In addition to these, the following more specialised brushes are useful: a small (No. 3) rigger is good for veining on larger paintings as it holds a lot of paint and does not need loading so often. I use a 13mm (½in) or 6mm (¼in) flat acrylic brush, which is a little firmer than a watercolour brush, for softening outlines and lifting out painted areas. A large wash brush will also come in handy to wet backgrounds; a No. 6 will suffice, but I use anything up to a No. 16.

Hair dryer

Masking fluid

Spray mister

Palette

━━ Other equipment

WATER CONTAINER I use ordinary jam jars to hold water.

SCISSORS You will need a good sharp pair of scissors.

PIPETTE This is useful when mixing the larger first washes. Pipettes cost little and make it easier to dilute a colour to the shade you require.

PENCIL SHARPENER Use this to sharpen pure graphite pencils.

OLD PAINTBRUSH AND DIP PEN An old brush is useful for applying masking fluid, but a dip pen when you want fine detail or lines.

DRAWING PINS These are useful when attaching your paper to a drawing board.

RULE OR STRAIGHT EDGE Use this for measuring paper and for drawing a border for your painting.

LARGE SOFT BRUSH Use this to brush away rubbed-off particles of masking fluid.

PLASTIC ERASER I prefer this to a putty eraser as it is a little firmer, and never takes the surface off the paper. To erase small or fiddly areas, cut a small slice off the end of your eraser to make a finer point.

KITCHEN PAPER Use these to adjust the moisture on brushes or to pick up droplets of paint or water.

MASKING TAPE Use this or gummed paper strip to attach lighter-weight papers to your drawing board when stretching paper.

HAIR DRYER This can be used to speed up the drying process, but I feel that it can dull the colours a little, and may also make masking fluid sticky and more difficult to remove. If you do use one, make sure the shine has gone off your painting before you start or it will move the paint.

MASKING FLUID Use this to mask off areas of your painting.

SPRAY MISTER This is ideal for softening pans of paint that have dried, or for spraying the paper to re-wet it if a wash has dried unevenly. Any empty domestic spray can be rinsed and filled with clean water.

PALETTE I use a white china palette for mixing colours. White is the best choice because you will be able to see the true colours, unchanged by any colour underneath. Some artists simply use large white china dinner plates or white plastic trays which you can obtain from hardware stores.

Not shown:

FOUNTAIN PEN I use a fountain pen to trace off an image, as pencil lines cannot be seen through carbon placed on a design.

BALLPOINT PEN I use a ballpoint pen when I am tracing off a design from carbon paper.

METHYLATED SPIRIT Use this with a pad or piece of cotton wool to even out carbon used for a tracing.

COLOUR & PAINT

USING WATERCOLOUR

Part of the joy of painting is the excitement of choosing and trying out new colours. I prefer to use mostly transparent colours, and much of the time I feel the brighter the better – as you will see from my paintings.

Many beginners are tempted to play it safe with watercolour, but I would urge you to frighten yourself when applying paint – it will dry lighter than it appears when freshly applied and when used wet-in-wet, it will diffuse and soften. As the old saying goes, 'if it's right when it's wet, it's wrong.'

I have not included a colour wheel in this section because I find them deceptive. There are so many variations in makes and shades that they can bear little resemblance to those featured in a basic colour wheel.

This part of the book looks at the techniques for preparing, mixing and using watercolour paint. I have included a few basic mixes to start you off which you should find useful, particularly if you are a beginner. As you become familiar with the mixes, you will begin to remember how they look.

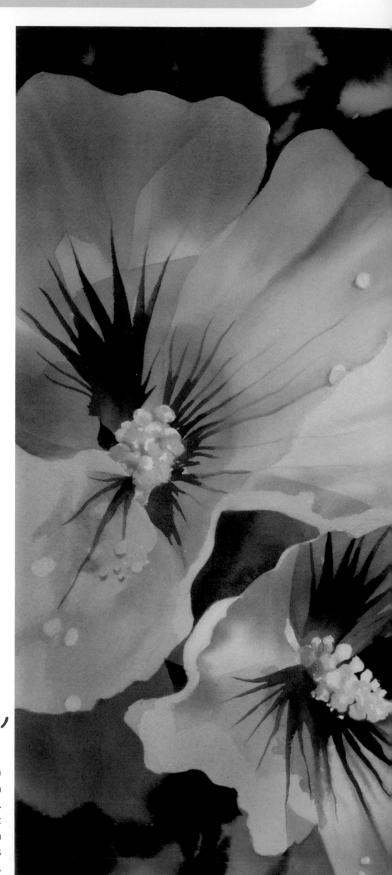

Hibiscus 'Bluebird'

93 x 75cm (36½ x 29½in)

These flowers appears to fade from deeper purple-blue through to lavender and then to white where areas catch the sun. The colours of hibiscus flowers make a lovely combination that is accentuated by the dark green background behind them When painting blue flowers, I often underpaint with pink. This underlayer glows through the blue glaze added on top.

▬ My basic palette

These are the colours I use at the moment. However, I like to experiment with different colours and my palette changes frequently. There are so many lovely colours available that I could not bear to use the same ones year after year.

   The technique I find best-suited to capturing the frailty of petals in sunshine is glazing – layering one colour over another dry colour. As a result, I favour transparent watercolours, which allow some of the underlying colour to show through.

   Note that using too many layers and colours can give a muddy result, so I would only glaze a couple of times to avoid this happening. The intense colours below combine well, but never be afraid to experiment; it takes time but is well worth the effort.

Cadmium red	Magenta	Permanent rose	Light red
Cobalt blue	Winsor blue	Winsor green	Sap green
Cadmium yellow	Aureolin	Golden ochre	Burnt umber	Indigo

Opposite:

Tulips

38 x 56cm (15 x 22in)

This vibrant painting uses shades from my basic palette including cadmium yellow, Winsor blue, cadmium red and permanent rose.

▬ Extra colours

Here are some colours that I frequently use alongside or in addition to my basic palette. While not essential, they are invaluable for making particular effects for specific flowers.

Transparent orange

For flowers and to warm foliage: there is a surprising amount of colour in grasses and leaves.

Red gold lake

This transparent golden colour can be used as a glaze to give depth to yellow flowers.

Purple

Endless variations are mixed with this versatile colour. Blues will cool it and permanent rose brighten it.

Cerulean blue

Mixed with cobalt or Winsor blue, this extends my range of blues for flowers such as meconopsis.

Rose 'Westerland'

54 x 44cm (21¼ x 17¼in)

As with the hibiscus flowers on pages 16–17, I have underpainted this rose. Starting with pink, I glazed gold and then orange over the area, following the tonal values to give it form and depth. I added purple shadows on the right-hand rose, to push it back a little. The dark centres are a gift as they immediately hold the attention and create focal points. I added flecks of light (easily masked out at the beginning) to them in order to give contrast and added interest.

JANET WHITLE

─ Basic mixes

Most of these mixes on these pages are used in the step-by-step demonstrations, but they are not the be-all and end-all. By all means try these out, but do not let them stop you experimenting to find your own preferred mixes. I am always discovering new mixes and I hope you will too.

The selection includes warm and cool mixes which are just as important for flowers as they are for landscapes, a fact that is often overlooked.

Permanent rose & aureolin	*Golden ochre & Winsor blue*	*Winsor blue & permanent rose*
This lovely transparent orange/salmon colour is useful for flowers including roses.	Unlike many greens, this good sage green will not dry dull and cold and spoil a lively painting.	These mix a really vibrant purple that does not dry flat, and will mix on the paper wet-in-wet.

Viridian, Winsor blue & magenta	*Burnt umber & viridian*
These intense colours mix a 'wonder dark' that never dries flat and dull.	This rich olive green is useful for the darks in foliage and leaves, without being dull.

Opposite:

Eryngium 'Sea Holly'

35 x 35cm (13¾ x 13¾in)

This eryngium was painted using a fairly limited palette of Winsor blue, viridian, and permanent rose. These were mixed to give the purples used as shadow colours. Some areas of clean white paper are left in the background give the painting a contrast in tones.

Tonal contrast is the best way to give depth to your paintings, and something I always aim for. This has to be planned in advance, as the white of the paper is used rather than white paint for the brightest tones. As a result, clean spaces must be left clean as you paint.

Shadow mixes

It is no exaggeration to say that shadows can make or break a painting. Shadows greatly affect the tonal contrast of the painting, and can change a mediocre work to one with great depth and interest. It is easy to overlook shadows, but as artists, we must observe them, as they provide atmosphere, which always makes a difference.

It is important not to use black paint for shadows, as it will have a deadening effect on your painting. Instead, mix a shadow colour, such as the examples shown opposite.

Shadows are often applied over the basic flower colour towards the end of a painting, although the order in which you work will vary with different flowers – this principle also applies to the centres of flowers.

Do not be timid in applying shadows. As with any layering you do in watercolour, it is best not to have to go in again, as things can start to get muddy very quickly. Make sure that the painting is bone dry, mix plenty of the shadow colour and apply the mix confidently.

Blackthorn

54 x 44cm (21¼ x 17¼in)

White flowers are a favourite of mine to paint. The soft shadowing on the petals in the background creates the cool atmosphere of an early spring day. The flowers blossom before the leaves appear, so there is little green to paint, but a few touches in the background washes alongside the deep browns of the branches help to bring shape and contrast to the composition. I lifted out indistinct shapes in the background with a damp brush, in order to suggest out-of-focus flowers.

JANET WHITTLE

Cobalt blue & permanent rose

This soft lilac is more effective for shadows than mixes with black, which can dry flat and lifeless.

Cobalt blue & light red

I tend to mix this warm grey with a slight bias towards the blue, as light red can be a dominant colour.

Tip

Drop in warm colour in cool shadows and cool in warm to give rich neutrals.

Greens

Greens can be very cold colours that become easily deadened. I suggest mixing intense, vibrant colours that can be calmed down, with a glaze of blue or purple if necessary. This will ensure the greens retain their luminosity and do not become flat or bland.

Lemon yellow & viridian

This is good to retain brightness in first washes. Glazed back, it gives a glow to grasses and leaves.

Winsor blue & viridian

Many leaves are this turquoise green. It is a useful first wash where there is a shine to the leaf.

Cadmium yellow & Winsor blue

These colours mix a wide range of greens from bright to dark depending on the amounts used.

Cadmium yellow & viridian

A richer, warmer green mix than with lemon yellow. I like to vary greens from cool to warm.

Cobalt blue & viridian

This gives a softer turquoise than the mix above, depending on the mood of your painting.

Troubleshooting

When using colour, there are several stumbling blocks that students commonly run up against. These include:

• **NOT SQUIRTING OUT ENOUGH COLOUR** Some of the most generous people I know are guilty of being mean with paint. I regularly come across students who are desperately trying to extract the last remnants of paint from a dried-up tube, or vainly trying to moisten a hard lump of paint that has been on their palette for months. You are just going to have to brace yourself, give in gracefully and try to enjoy it.

• **NOT MIXING THE COLOURS BRIGHTLY ENOUGH** When working wet-in-wet, as I do a great deal, remember that the colour will diffuse and spread, and that watercolour will dry lighter. The general rule is: 'If it's right when it's wet, then it's wrong!'

• **NOT MIXING ENOUGH PAINT** You will not have time to mix more paint while you are in the middle of applying a wash. Always mix more than you think you will need, and you are likely to find that you have mixed just the right amount. If there is some left over, it will not be wasted because you will need the colours throughout the painting.

Tip

In hot weather, watercolour can be a difficult medium, especially when putting in large washes, as the heat makes them dry at different rates. Adding a few drops of ox gall fluid to your washes helps the flow and promotes even drying.

Cabbage White on Syringa Blossom

38 x 56cm (15 x 22in)

Using a limited palette makes you explore one colour and take it to its limits without being sidetracked by different colours. I used the whole tonal range from white to darkest green to give the depth needed.

JANET WHITTLE

Using a limited palette

The phrase 'limited palette' indicates a conscious decision to restrict the colours you use. For example, you might restrict yourself to just three colours for the whole painting. The approach is not one that I commonly choose to use in my own painting, although it may be yours when you have evolved your own style.

Composition is the most important part of a successful painting. Colour, although very important, comes second for me. However, if the colour was the main thing that attracted you to a flower and provided you with your inspiration, then follow your instinct in the painting. The lilies shown here, for example, were such a rich and wonderful colour I decided very little else was needed to portray them, so the painting was executed using very few colours: transparent orange, translucent yellow, aureolin, alizarin crimson, Indian red and Winsor blue.

There are a lot of tonal changes in this painting so you have to decide which flowers to push and pull to make an interesting composition. While the palette was mostly warm orangey-red colours, including the complementary (Winsor blue) allowed me to create the interesting dark tones. Getting the depth of colour with a limited palette still relies on glazing; this must still be done carefully as even one colour can become the dreaded mud if you are not careful in your application of the paint.

Lilies 'Red Night'

52 x 33cm (20½ x 13in)

This is a good example of a painting done with a limited palette (see also *Cabbage White on Syringa Blossom*, page 27). I masked out the stamen and used the full tonal range of white through orange to burnt orange, taking the colour to dark by adding burnt umber. These flowers are often sold in pots, making it easy for the painter to position them where the light is best. As the petals have a sheen on them, I have used the white of the paper to represent the sunlight catching them. The veining on the petals was put in using a small rigger brush.

▬ Palette swaps

Colour is often what will initially attract the viewer to a painting, and the variety of colours you have to choose from when painting flowers is amazing. In fact, it is so broad that it is entirely possible that you will have reference of flowers that are ideal in composition, but are not the colour you want to paint. In these cases, you can simply change the colour, as with the examples on these pages, which were both based on the same reference photographs.

  Once you make the decision to change the colours, it can be tricky to know where to start. Happily, there are various techniques and tools to hand in order to help guide you. If you bear in mind that the background colour, size of the flowers, and the size and shape of your composition are important to the overall effect, you will quickly see that there is a lot of guidance that does not wholly rely on the colour you choose, so you can begin with some confidence. There is no need to reinvent the wheel - only replace what you need to.

  If you do decide to change the colours of the flowers in your painting, check that the species does occur in the colour you wish to paint first. With so many varieties of flowers, it is likely there is at least one that is close to the colour you wish to use.

Hydrangea 'Aspera'

73 x 56cm (28¾ x 22in)

Consistent tone

Changing the colour you use should not affect the tone - this aspect of the image should remain largely the same. Dark areas will still be dark, and highlights remain light; as demonstrated in the two images below, which are simply the main paintings with the colour stripped out - notice how similar they appear. When mixing your new colours, therefore, pay particular attention to the tones you create.

Hydrangea 'Blue Wave'

73 x 56cm (28¾ x 22in)

Tip

Bigger is not always better. With the right background and composition, small flowers, such as those shown on these pages, are very effective in their own right as a subject.
They also work fantastically well as a foil to larger flowers. They create a different texture and add interest.

GETTING

STARTED

DRAWING

When I have not painted a particular flower before, I always find it helpful to do a detailed drawing before I start to paint so I can familiarise myself with the flower, its form and shape, and how it grows. If, when I come to paint, the flower is no longer in bloom or there are gaps in my reference material, this information can be used to bridge any gaps.

Why make an initial drawing?

I find that if a composition does not work in pencil it does not work in paint. Drawing a flower helps me to understand the form, and I can experiment with composition because errors can be erased easily. When I come to do the painting I am halfway there.

I usually start with a simple line drawing of the composition, like the ones shown at the beginning of the demonstrations in this book. I keep the line light and put in the first tone, leaving white for highlights.

I prefer to work over my whole drawing rather than finishing one part and moving on to the next because I think it helps to pull everything together.

Convolvulus

The dark leaf shapes bring the white flower forward, but do not do this all round the flower as it makes the composition heavy. Pick out one or two areas, and the eye will fill in the rest.

Tone and outline

In the real world there are very few actual lines, just changes in tone. For this reason, it is important to dispense with lines and learn to shade these changes of tone as soon as possible. When I am drawing, I gradually work darker using a 3B or 4B pencil, going over some of the lighter tone and feathering it in.

If you want a particular part of a drawing or painting to appear to come forward or show up, darken behind it. Beginners often outline aspects of a drawing or painting hoping to achieve this, but all it does is make the flower look heavy.

I put in the darks to give depth to the composition using a 9B pencil. Make sure that you place the darkest darks against the lightest lights, a process known as counterchanging.

Iris

In this drawing I have darkened the stem beneath the front petal. The result is that it appears to be coming closer towards you.

JANET WHITTLE

My initial drawing

Using your drawings

A completed drawing can be traced and lightly transferred on to your watercolour paper where it will serve as a guide when painting. The original drawing can be used as a tonal guide for the painting, too.

This drawing was done on cartridge paper using an HB pencil for the outline, then a mixture of HB, 3B, 6B and 9B pencils. I put in the darks last.

When I have finished a drawing I usually spray it with fixative to stop any smudging. This does not prevent me from adding more pencil later if I think it is necessary.

Tip

Drawing is more controllable than painting because you can erase, so it will help to build your confidence.

Fuchsia

38 x 56cm (15 x 22in)

This was done on 640gsm (300lb) Not paper using the drawing to the left as a guide. The main flowers were masked and a mixture of greens, blues and pinks were dropped into the background. The leaves were brought forward with negative painting - see page 56. The flowers were painted last, using the blues from the background to shadow the white petals, and a mixture of permanent rose, cadmium red and cadmium yellow for the other petals.

Tulips

33 x 33cm (13 x 13in)

Drawing and painting in the same composition is a lovely and very effective technique. A smooth paper (cold-pressed) has been used here as it is easier to draw on. I make a preliminary sketch, draw in a circle and mask out beyond it using masking fluid. When the painting is dry, I remove the masking fluid, then complete the drawing with a variety of pencils.

Daffodils

33 x 33cm (13 x 13in)

This painting uses the same paper and technique as for *Tulips* (opposite). A set of paintings using the same technique but different subjects can be appealing. You might also like to try varying the shape behind the flowers, using a square or an oval.

Stretching paper

I usually stretch all my paper, with the exception of 640gsm (300lb). Sometimes I even stretch this, but perhaps I was born a pessimist! The wet-in-wet washes I use can cockle the paper, and this will always show under a mount.

There are ways to flatten paper after it has been painted on, but I feel they are fraught with more problems than they are worth. The heavier the paper the less likely it is to cockle, as long as the washes are not too wet. I find that the painting which cockles the worst is always the best one you have done in a long while, and you will often regret not having taken the trouble to stretch the paper. The choice is yours!

When you are stretching paper, the heavier the weight of paper the longer it will need to be immersed in water. For example, 190gsm (90lb) will need only around two minutes but 640gsm (300lb) will need three or four minutes. Take care not to soak the paper for too long though, as this will change the way it reacts to your washes and may cause problems.

How to stretch paper

1 You will need a drawing board, the paper you want to stretch and some gummed brown paper strip 38-50mm (½in) wide. Make sure your drawing board is approximately 10cm (4in) larger all round than the paper. The whole sheet of paper must be immersed or it will be unevenly soaked. I find the best way is to run a shallow bath and immerse several sheets at once, but remember that you will need a drawing board for every piece of paper.

2 When the paper is soaked, remove it from the water and tip it to one side to allow the excess to run off. Lay it on your drawing board and pat it with absorbent paper, or a tea towel, to remove the shine. Tear off four strips of gummed tape a little longer than the sides of your paper. Draw them through the water one at a time, removing the excess water by running the strip through your fingers.

3 Lay the first strip half on the drawing board and half on the paper to fix it down, and smooth it lightly to remove air bubbles. Repeat on all four sides. To provide more stability when using a very large sheet of paper, drawing pins can be used over the top of the tape in each of the four corners.

4 Leave the board to dry flat: this is important because if you stand it up, the water will drain to the bottom and the paper will dry unevenly, increasing the chances of it pulling away from the tape.

5 When the painting is finished, you can remove it from the board by slitting between the paper and the brown tape.

Tip

Make sure the strips of brown paper are fixed evenly to your drawing board: if one side is stronger it may pull away from the others. If you find your paper is not fixed evenly, all is not lost: soak or cut it off and start again.

Transferring designs

Making transfer paper

Making your own tracing-down paper is easy, and allows you to transfer your own designs or sketches to watercolour paper. I use a fountain pen to trace the design but a black felt-tip pen is fine too. Methylated spirit is used to 'scumble' the pencil marks, which sets the graphite and covers the back of the design evenly with carbon. The advantage of this method is that the tracing-down paper can be used many times. If you are not happy with your first painting you will not have to start completely from scratch; this will give you more confidence.

   If you want to make sure your design does not slip while you are transferring it to your watercolour paper, lay the tracing-down paper on the paper you have drawn your design on and attach it to the top with 'hinges' of masking tape.

You will need

· Tracing paper
· A pen with black ink
· Soft pencil (9B)
· Methylated spirit
· Cotton wool pad
· Watercolour paper
· Masking tape
· Ballpoint pen

1   Lay the tracing paper over your design and trace it using a fountain pen and black ink.

2   Turn the tracing paper over and use a soft pencil (9B) to scribble evenly over the back of the design.

3   With a cotton wool pad and a small amount of methylated spirit, 'scumble' the pencil marks. Leave it to dry.

4   Turn the tracing paper over and lay it on your watercolour paper, fixing it with hinges of masking tape. Use a ballpoint pen to trace the design.

5   Check to make sure that the design has come through before removing the tape hinges. If necessary, replace them and re-trace any areas that are too faint, adding more carbon if necessary.

The design shown in these steps is for the rose painting – the finished painting can be seen on page 49.

Tip

If the tracing paper moves or the 'hinges' of tape come off, stick the point of a pin in a recognisable place, such as the intersection of two lines. Then put the point of the pin in the same spot in your unfinished tracing and realign it. Re-attach the tape hinges.

Using photocopies

The simplest way of transferring a design is by using a photocopy of something you like. The advantage of this method is that it can be enlarged or reduced to suit the size of painting you wish to produce.

To transfer a design using a photocopy, scribble in soft pencil on the back of the photocopy and transfer the image (see page 41). You cannot use methylated spirit to even out and 'set' the pencil marks, so take care not to lean on your work or the graphite may rub off and make your paper grey.

You can also make a plain carbon sheet to use between the photocopy and your watercolour paper. Do this by scribbling on tracing paper with a soft pencil (9B) and 'scumbling' with methylated spirits as on page 41.

Opposite:

Irises

38 x 56cm (15 x 22in)

These irises were white, but as previously mentioned, the amount of white in apparently white flowers is often very little! I used quite a vibrant purple/violet for the shadows and tonal values, and also dropped it in to the background to unite the painting. Softer shapes of flowers have been cut out to give it depth. As purple and orange are complementary colours, these were emphasised as much as possible for effect. To give the painting vitality, the focal flowers were counterchanged towards the centre by placing the darkest darks against the lightest lights.

Using a grid

A grid is another effective way to transfer a design to watercolour paper. Divide your original drawing or sketch into quarters or eighths (depending on the size) and copy one square at a time onto your paper. Erase the pencilled grid lines before you begin to paint as they can be confusing.

COMPOSITION

It is important to spend time on composition before you start to paint. The less experience you have with painting, the more you will need to plan ahead. A well-composed painting is much more likely to be successful than one you rush into, and it will be more enjoyable to work upon as you paint.

Not all artists draw first, but those who are brave enough not to do so are those with the experience to keep the basic composition in their heads and adjust elements as they go along. I find that producing one or two thumbnail sketches before I begin to paint is usually enough to inspire me.

Starting points

If you are not sure where to start, work through this list to get your thoughts flowing and organise your plan of action.

- If you are not painting from life, collect together all the reference material you have on the type of flower or flowers you wish to paint.

- Decide which type of paper and which shape of painting – for example, portrait, landscape or letterbox (see opposite) – suits your subject best.

- Make thumbnail sketches to decide the position of the main flowers.

- Draw a border to contain your composition: it makes it easier to visualise.

- Draw your design, either by tracing it from cartridge paper to watercolour paper or, as your confidence grows, straight on to the paper.

- Decide the direction of the light and stick to it throughout your painting. Your finished painting will look extremely odd if you have light coming from different directions.

- Remember to interlock some shapes to avoid 'holes' in the middle of your composition.

- Vary the size of different elements of your painting, taking care to include buds, half- and fully opened flowers, and different sized leaves. If all elements are the same size the effect will be like wallpaper.

- Mask out areas where appropriate.

- Choose your palette, and remember artistic licence means you can change the colour of the flowers and the background.

- Think beautiful thoughts!

JANET WHITLE

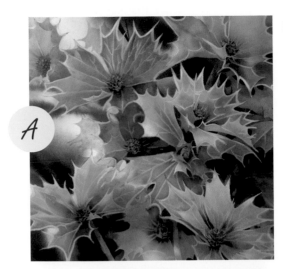

Start planning

One of the earliest decisions you need to make is the format of the painting, which determines the shape of the finished piece. The images on this page show some common formats for painting, though there also more unusual options – like a circular or oval composition – that you might like to try.

Common painting formats
A: square; B: portrait; C: landscape; D: letterbox.

▬▬ Thumbnail sketches

When making thumbnail sketches to decide the position of the main flowers, there is no need to go into any detail at this stage; be looser, with simple shapes to determine the size and direction of the focal flowers and the main leaves and stalks.

Then you may change your mind several times without feeling you have to stick with your original drawing as you spent a lot of time on it.

Also sketch in where you want some of the background flowers as you may want to put colours in your first wash in order to do some negative painting to bring them out in your second background wash.

When drawing on your watercolour paper, scale up your chosen thumbnail sketch by dividing it into quarters: that way you will not be tempted to draw smaller.

A selection of quick thumbnail sketches made to explore various potential formats for a painting. Clockwise from top right: landscape, square, circular, portrait, letterbox.

Vignettes

Vignettes offer another option when you are composing your painting. These paintings do not have a defined border or edge. Instead, they simply fade into the background.

To do this, just wet the area of the paper where you want paint to go. You are in control because the paint will go only where you have used water. Draw your composition with an HB pencil, mask out the main flowers if you wish, and wet the background up to the masking but leaving a broken edge. Drop the paint in and tip the board so that it flows into the shapes you have made with the clear water.

This part-worked vignette (the complete version is detailed overleaf) shows how the background colours are blended away to nothing using clean water.

JANET WHITTLE

Using photographs

I paint mainly from life, but I find photographs invaluable. In an ideal world, flowers would not wilt or die until you had finished painting them, and the sun would shine all the time. As this is not the case, good reference photographs can be a real asset when you want to paint intricate flowers. Digital cameras make gathering reference images very simple, making it easier for you to print out photographs that are successful and inspire you to paint.

Flowers change very rapidly, especially in the summer months. Not many of us get the time to have long periods painting and sketching from life, so photographic reference is invaluable – and the more the better: choice is everything.

The example opposite shows how the best aspects of two photographs can be used to produce a study, not a slavish copy. The background is a very simple vignette, and the leaves are painted dark against light.

What to photograph

Try to capture the flowers from all angles and at all stages of development so that you have the best possible scope for your composition. To aid your memory, take a few good close-ups of details. Do not just photograph the petals – buds and leaves are important supporting elements in your painting, so do be sure to include these when gathering reference.

Light direction

In flower painting, as with landscapes, the direction of light must be consistent or the result will be confused. When you take reference photographs, make sure the subject is lit from the same direction in each. Take several at the same time of day to ensure your painting is consistently lit from the same direction. Shadows should not be painted with some in the afternoon and some in the evening as this will look odd to the viewer.

Tip

I file my photographs in boxes in alphabetical order so particular flowers are easy to find.

Rose

27 x 35cm (10½ x 13¾in)
To add more texture at the edges I have used a spatter technique – flicking paint off the tip of a flat brush over the painting. If you try this, make sure the first wash is dry and cover the flowers before you start to spatter.

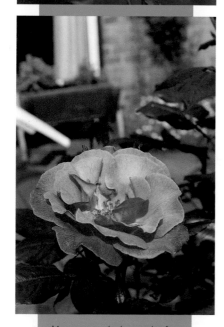

My source photographs for the painting opposite.

TECHNIQUES

As you become more experienced with different watercolour techniques, it is a common mistake to try to incorporate too many in a painting. Different approaches suit different flowers, so you should try to imagine how your subject would look best, and use the most suitable technique to enable you to achieve the effect.

In the following section of the book, I describe the techniques I use most so that you can practise and decide for yourself. Over the following pages I will take you step by step through these exciting techniques and give you plenty of practice so that you can tackle the projects later in the book with confidence. I hope you enjoy them.

Putting in a background

This exercise is extremely good practice, and there are no hard-and-fast rules: it starts with just an idea that you have in your head. Imagine the colours of the flowers, leaves and sunlight. Mix the colours you have imagined, wet the paper and drop them in.

Tip the board to let the colours merge and leave it to dry, or wait until the shine has gone off and dry your work with a hair dryer.

Next, use the shapes that have settled in your wash and draw your composition on top, making the most of happy accidents: every wash will be different!

The next step is to paint the negative shapes behind the flowers in a slightly darker tone, just to 'find' your composition. If any of the colours are not what you want, you can change them by glazing other transparent colours over the top (see page 60).

Put in the colours and tip the painting while they remain wet (see above), and encourage them to merge and blend.

Poppies

55 x 38cm (21½ x 15in)

For the background of this painting, I used an approach that is great fun. I did not draw a composition on the paper before I began, but just flooded in the colours of the flowers and foliage. I tipped my drawing board so the colours merged and blended in the usual way, then let it all dry to see how they settled on the page. Then I drew the composition on top of the wash. This is really good practice for negative painting (see page 56), because you paint behind the flowers, stalks and leaves to make them appear.

Wet-in-wet and wet-on-dry

Wet-in-wet is one of the basic watercolour techniques, and one that is well worth practising until you get the timing right. It is exactly what it sounds like – applying wet paint to wet paper. The skill lies in dampening the paper evenly, and dropping in the colours at the right time to diffuse where you want them to. Wet colours will mix on the wet paper and result in soft edges that can later be sharpened by negative painting or left, depending on how your washes turned out. This is where watercolour has 'happy accidents' that can be utilised as you progress through the painting.

This exercise combines wet-in-wet and wet-on-dry, the techniques I use most. Mask the three main flowers completely – not just round the edges – and wet the background paper up to the masking, taking care not to leave gaps. Drop in your chosen colours. The three washes I used (viridian and Winsor blue; cadmium yellow and indigo, and Winsor blue) have blended in places to create other colours. The blues are used for the background flowers. Let this wet-in-wet stage dry completely before going on.

When your first wash is dry, draw some additional flowers and leaves in the background with a 2B or 3B pencil. Then, with the same colours as for the first washes, paint wet-on-dry behind these additional flowers and leaves – a technique also known as cutting out. Though the paper behind these shapes is dry, you should keep a wet edge to the paint so you do not leave hard lines: load the brush so the paint leaves it easily and you do not have to spread it on. When an area is evenly damp, you can also drop in other colours, just as you do with a first wash.

Wet-in-wet
Working wet paint into wet paint will allow the colours to bleed into one another for smooth results.

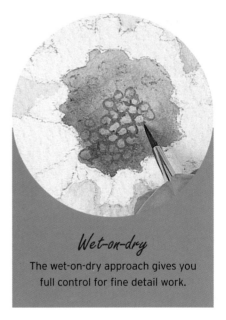

Wet-on-dry
The wet-on-dry approach gives you full control for fine detail work.

My outline sketch for this painting

Opposite:

Daisies

28 x 38cm (11 x 15in)

The centres of the background flowers are merely an indication, with little detail. The background was allowed to dry, then the masking was removed from the three focal flowers and the petals shaded with cobalt blue. The centres were painted using lemon yellow, then while the paint was still wet cadmium red was touched in on the side away from the light so it softened into the yellow. A touch of blue was added to darken one side, and the stalks were put in using a mixture of lemon yellow and cobalt blue.

Peony 'Alba Plena'

55 x 40cm (21½ x 15¾in)
Worked wet-in-wet, I used a flower mister to dampen the paper for this fresh-looking effect. You can also do this using a well-rinsed empty plastic spray bottle or a sponge.

Tip

Discarded painting paper is never wasted: mix up your colours and practise the wet-in-wet or glazing techniques on off-cuts or failed attempts so that you are not afraid to try them on a painting that is going well, or near completion. Often the last minutes of work can make or break a painting, transforming it from mediocre to good or – fingers crossed – brilliant!

Opposite:

Poppies

52 x 33cm (20½ x 13in)
The red of the poppies was dropped in to the background wash and then 'cut out' with the next wash to make background flowers that fill out the composition and give another depth to the painting. Sunlight bleaches out colour and details, so on some of the edges of the focal flowers I have let the colour bleed out to the white of the paper to bring a lightness to the petals, as though the sunlight is catching them. The leaves and stalks were brought forward by painting in negative shapes, a technique I use often in my painting.

Negative painting

Negative painting is a wonderful technique for picking out shapes in the background washes, and can be used for flowers or for leaves and stalks. If your background wash is quite dark you may need to reinstate your pencil guidelines before you begin. A 3B pencil is the best type to use for this as it does not dent the paper, and is more visible over a colour.

When you have done this, mix up more of the colours you have used for the background washes, and paint negative shapes – that is, the spaces and gaps around the positive shapes – behind the flowers and leaves you want to show up. Keep the effect soft and simple to ensure that the negative flowers complement rather than compete with your focal flowers. Do not add too much detail at this stage as it tends to bring things forward: you can add detail later if necessary.

Let your work dry, then plan and put in more leaf and flower shapes within the first layer of negative shapes. This gives more depth to the painting. These shapes should also be painted in negative, using a darker tone to produce a three-dimensional effect. It may sound complicated, but it will become easier with a little practice.

Clematis

Below: 70 x 55cm (27½ x 20½in)
Right: 80 x 70cm (31½ x 27½in)

The paintings on these pages show two ways of approaching the same flower: you should always choose the colours and style of painting you feel happiest with. The painting on the right shows a more colourful, vibrant approach, while the one below is more ethereal and gentle.

Hard and soft edges

Hard and soft edges or, as they are sometimes called, lost and found, are a very important part of painting. Too many hard edges can make a composition look overworked and bitty, so it is best to vary the type of edges. At first, I like to keep most of the edges within the flowers soft, using the wet-in-wet technique. When the painting is almost finished, I assess whether any part of the image needs to be sharpened.

   If you want to control a soft edge within a small shape, for example a petal, paint in the deeper-toned area first. Rinse your brush, then paint up to the edge with clear water. This makes the colour bleed forward, and creates a soft edge that is more controllable.

Softening outside edges
It is easier to remove paint from some papers than others, and you will have to discover which you prefer by trying out different papers. With most papers, however, you can soften hard edges that have been produced by masking out by dampening a small flat brush and rubbing gently across the edge. Synthetic bristles are best for this as they are a little firmer. Blot with a tissue to remove any excess moisture.

   In the examples shown below, which are part of the *Snowdrops* demonstration that begins on page 66, a flat brush has been used to rub the edges of the masked areas to soften them, so they look less 'cut out'.

Using a flat brush dampened with clear water, gently rub the edge of the adjacent coloured area to soften it and blot with soft tissue.

Repeat with the rest of the flowers, neatening any jagged edges.

'Godaishu'

55 x 38cm (21½ x 15in)

I have used hard and soft edges to paint this peony. Too much detail would make the flower form confusing to the eye. The main areas of counterchange - where the lightest lights are next to the darkest darks - have been accentuated in the middle and on the outside edges.

Glazing

Glazing is a technique that can be used to warm up or cool down areas of a painting, and the best results are obtained with washes of transparent colour. If leaves or stalks look dull or pale, a light wash of aureolin or lemon yellow will brighten them. A cobalt blue glaze will help to accentuate focal flowers by cooling or pushing back surrounding areas. In the example below (see also page 106) the glazing gives definition and shape to the daisy petals.

The daisies look too stark because they are just white paper (above) but glazing with a pale wash of cobalt blue when the flowers are dry helps to give them definition, as seen below.

Wisteria

55 x 38cm (21½ x 15in)

In this example, some of the flowers have been glazed back with a purple mix to make the focal flowers more prominent.

JANET WHITTLE

Lifting out

Some papers allow you to lift off paint more easily than others. On certain types of paper, if you are not happy with the way your first wash has gone on, all you need to do to remove it is to rinse your work off under a tap and scrub it gently with a brush. Some types of paint leave more of a stain on the paper, so that a light blush of colour will always remain, while others can be removed completely allowing you to start again. Beginners should experiment with different paints and papers to find which ones suit different techniques.

If you want to remove definite shapes, dampen the area first with clear water, then rub the shape gently with a brush and blot it with tissue (this technique can be seen to the left). For larger areas, a soft toothbrush can be used. If, when your work has dried, you find that you want to lift out more colour you can simply repeat the procedure.

You should also take care if you want to use masking fluid over colour. Because it is a rubber solution, certain types may lift off some of the colour when you try to remove it, as well as some of your pencil lines.

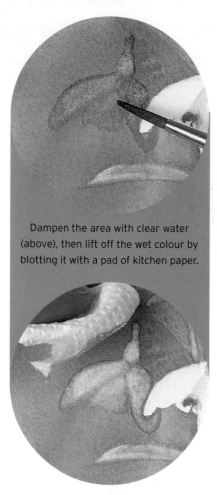

Dampen the area with clear water (above), then lift off the wet colour by blotting it with a pad of kitchen paper.

Lifting out stamens and stalks

Lifting out is a useful technique for putting in the stalks of flowers, as in the painting to the left. In the painting of hollyhocks opposite, negative painting was used to indicate the stalks, and the stamens were masked. You can apply a first wash before masking if you like, so there is a base colour when you remove the masking fluid.

When stamens are light against dark, including hellebores (see pages 64-65), or some types of clematis (see pages 56-57), it is easier to mask them out before you begin to paint.

When the stamens of flowers are dark against light, they can be painted in last over the colours of the flower. This technique is quite easy - see step 12 of the poppy demonstration on page 106 for an example.

Bowl of Beauty

28 x 38cm (11 x 15in)

The main stalks on these peony flowers were lifted out using a 13mm (½in) flat brush to give the impression that they run behind the leaves. A stalk was painted dark against light in the background.

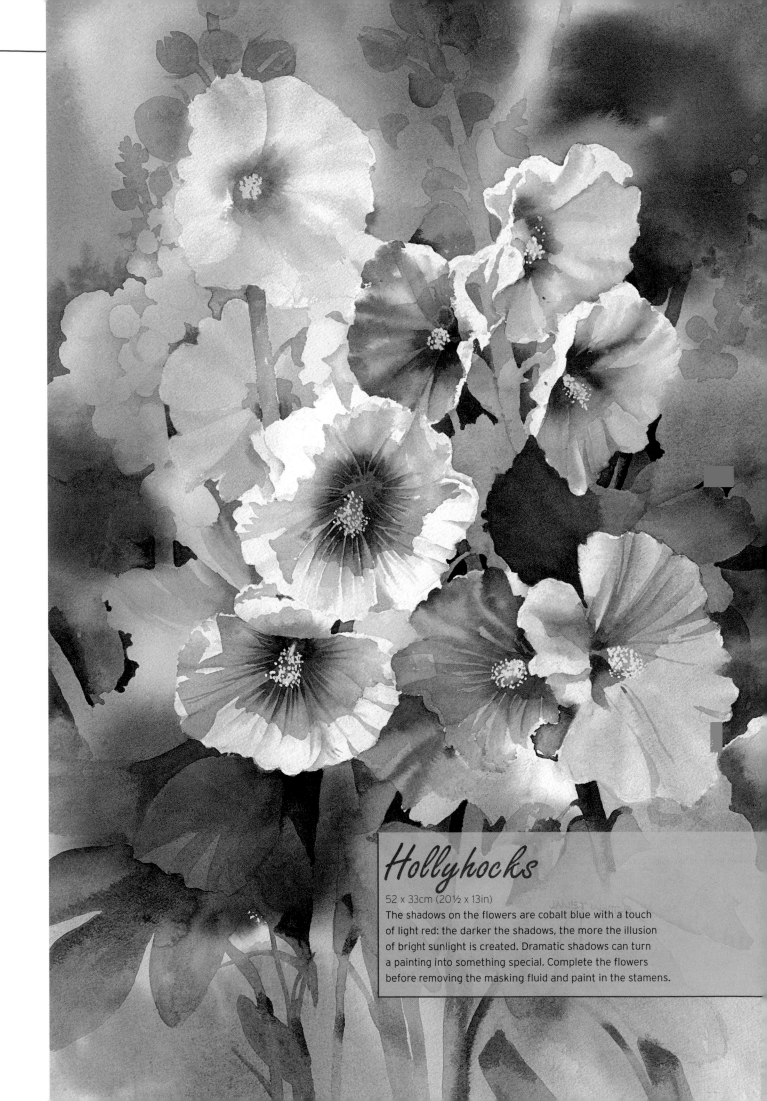

Hollyhocks

52 x 33cm (20½ x 13in)

The shadows on the flowers are cobalt blue with a touch of light red: the darker the shadows, the more the illusion of bright sunlight is created. Dramatic shadows can turn a painting into something special. Complete the flowers before removing the masking fluid and paint in the stamens.

Using masking fluid

Some masking fluid lifts off the colours underneath, so it is a good idea to experiment with different makes. Use a dip pen or an old brush and work a little neat soap into it first so the masking fluid washes out easily.

If you want to use masking fluid with a pen to produce narrow lines but it seems too thick, it can usually be diluted with a few drops of water. Masking fluid can also be used over a first wash, so that when you rub it off the paper underneath is already coloured. Try this over a blue wash when you are painting bluebells. If you find it difficult to see the masking fluid against the paper, mix in a small quantity of either ultramarine blue or cobalt blue as these colours will not stain the paper.

Make sure your masking fluid is not too old as it will have become thicker and harder to use. Some papers do not take masking fluid: it can soak in too much to remove later and will ruin your painting. Be careful to test your paper and masking fluid beforehand on a spare piece of the same paper as you will work your painting upon.

Flower centres

When painting flowers with a background the petals will show up easily, so there no need to overwork them as the lighter the touch the better, but the centres will need reinforcing with maybe two or three layers to give the depth of colour needed also the denote the direction the flower is facing.

The centres of flowers often have delicate details. If the central details are light against dark, as in the hellebores shown here, masking fluid can make the job much easier. Even if the centres are dark against light (as with the poppies on page 55), a few flecks of white created with masking fluid will add to the interest. You can easily remove them if not needed later.

Brush care

If allowed to dry on the bristles, masking fluid will quickly clog up your brushes. Working your brush over a piece of wet soap will protect it somewhat, but it is generally better to use an old or dedicated brush (such as the synthetic brush shown here) to apply masking fluid, and keep your best brushes away from it!

Hellebores

55 x 38cm (21½ x 15in)

Permanent rose was used underneath to give a glow to the darker colour of the flowers. The stamens were masked and painted last.

━━ Veining

The technique you use will depend on the type of flower or leaf you are painting: some have light veining against a dark background while others are dark against light. Do not add veining to all the petals, as it can be too much. The sun will also bleach out details. It is usually sufficient to vein just a few focal petals and leaves.

   Unless you want a botanical illustration, it is unnecessary to add too much detail to leaves or petals. Concentrate on the focal flowers to make them stand out more.

Dark veining against light

For dark veining against a light background, I use a small round brush (No. 00) or a small (No. 3) rigger, and paint in the vein following the contours of the leaf or petal. If there are any cast shadows, I put these in on top and darken the veining within the shadow.

Light veining against dark

For light veining against dark, you can mask out the veins over the colour of the background (see page 64 for more information on masking) then add another wash over the top. Alternatively, you can draw them in and paint the negative shapes carefully between them.

Tip

When you are painting a larger picture, use a small rigger (No. 2 or No. 3) for veining. The hairs are longer and will hold more paint, and you will not have to reload the brush so often.

Peonies 'Sarah Bernhardt'

52 x 33cm (20½ x 13in)

This is a simple treatment of an extremely intricate flower, with the sunlight catching the petals from above left. I have been sparing with the amount of veining so the effect did not become too complicated, but have deepened the veining within the shadow areas.

Butterflies

To add an extra touch of colour and interest to paintings, butterflies are ideal. The technique is easy, and you can practise different butterflies on odd pieces of watercolour paper. Mask out the outline and any white areas carefully and put in a simple wash of the main colour, for example red or yellow. Allow your work to dry, then put in the dark areas, stippling the paint in fine dots with the point of a small brush.

Peacock butterfly on cow parsley

Comma butterfly on a dahlia

Painted lady on Welsh poppies

Red Admiral butterfly on buddleia

SPIDER'S WEB

A cobweb can make a stunning addition to a flower painting. This exercise is really just a background, painted following the method shown on page 50, plus some masking fluid. Think of it as a warm-up and practice exercise for the flower paintings later in the book.

You can use any colours you like for this practice piece as you will not be adding flowers this time – part of the fun is seeing how it turns out! Draw the cobweb on your paper first. Reference photographs will help with this, but as every web is unique, you can use your imagination!

Some areas of the web have been glazed using cobalt blue, and some using lemon yellow. Other areas have been left white as though the sun is catching the web.

Tip

If you cannot find a flower or cobweb to photograph that still has the dew on it, use a spray mister to make it show up.

The photographs I used as reference for this painting

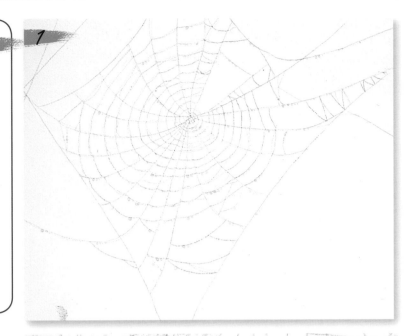

You will need

- Watercolour paper, 28 x 38cm (11 x 15in): you can use any weight, but remember to stretch lighter weight paper
- Pencil
- Dip pen or small brush
- Masking fluid
- Round brush No. 7
- Watercolour paints: choose a complementary combination of light and dark colours

1 Pin or stretch your paper to your drawing board and draw a spider's web. Remember that the weight of dew pulls the threads down, so curve the lines gently.

2 Go over the outlines of your drawing with masking fluid, using a dip pen or small brush, letting it form blobs of varying sizes to represent dew.

3 Mix the colours you want to use, then dampen the paper with a mister or brush. Begin to put on the paint, using a No. 7 brush, over the masking fluid as if you were just painting a background.

4 Build up the colour, painting gently so that you do not lift off the masking fluid lines from the paper.

5 Add in some bright tones.

6 Put in some darker tones.

7 Push the paint gently over the masking fluid lines so that there are no gaps.

8 Finally, drop in some very dark tones, and tip the board to blend the colours.

9 When the paper begins to dry, stop adding paint or the colours will not blend properly.

10 Tip your painting to merge the colours. Leave your work to dry,

11 Remove the masking fluid and paint in the dewdrops using a pale wash of cobalt blue, leaving a small highlight on each.

The finished painting can be seen on pages 70-71.

COW PARSLEY

The masking fluid technique is useful for flowers which have tiny florets, including forget-me-nots. The exercise on the following pages is good practice for putting in backgrounds and using masking fluid, and can be done with very little drawing. As the flower is white, you can use any colours you choose for the background.

Tip

Masking fluid can be used over an initial wash and another wash can be added over the top.

Masking fluid enabled me to keep areas of paper clean and white for the florets.

You will need

- Watercolour paper: you can use any weight but stretch lighter weight papers
- Watercolour paints of your choice: see the colours I used below
- Round brush No. 8
- Flat brush 13mm (½in)
- Small brush No. 00
- 3B pencil
- Masking fluid and dip pen or old brush

Before you begin to paint

Mix the colours you want to use. For this demonstration, I used cadmium red, lemon yellow, cobalt blue and sap green, and a dark mix of burnt umber and Winsor blue for the details on the butterfly.

The photographs I used as reference for this painting

1 Pencil in a border and lightly draw in the shape of the cow parsley. Mask out the flower heads, stalks and the butterfly outline and let it dry. Wet the whole of the paper and, using the flat brush, drop in the yellow, blue and green. Tip the paper to merge the colours. When you are happy with the effect, leave to dry.

2 When the first washes are dry, paint the background shadow of the cow parsley using the No. 8 round brush and blue. Mask out the tiny white dots on the wings of the butterfly, allow it to dry and put in a red wash over the top. Leave your work to dry.

3 Remove the masking on the stalks and put a wash of pale green, with highlights in yellow, over them.

4 Remove the masking fluid from the flowers and add a wash of lemon yellow to some of them, varying the tones.

5 Stipple in the dark areas of the butterfly using a mix of burnt umber and Winsor blue. Use the point of a small brush (No. 00) to paint the colour in small dots, which gives the effect of a subtle blend of colour rather than a hard edge.

6 Allow your work to dry. If you want to add any extra flecks of white to the background or butterfly wings, they can be scraped out with the tip of a scalpel.

The finished painting can be seen on pages 76-77.

FLOWERS

TO PAINT

JANET WHITLE

Project
SNOWDROPS

These have lovely, simple shapes to practise masking-out techniques on. Because they are so small, you will need to mask out the whole flower so the first washes can be put on over them. Draw the flower heads and stems carefully before you begin painting. You can draw the leaves in at this stage too, or you can leave them until you have completed the first wash if you prefer.

This project is a good exercise for practising a background wash, and also incorporates the lifting out technique. The colours were chosen because some pigments will lift off back to white, while others are more staining and leave some colour on the paper. It was carried out on watercolour board, which you can buy in most good art shops. This allows the paint to lift off more easily.

Make sure you choose your paper according to the techniques you are hoping to use. A surface which lifts off as easily as watercolour board is not suitable if you want to do a lot of negative painting; unless it is done extremely gently, it will lift off the colour underneath and make it muddy. The negative shapes in this composition are small, so this characteristic should not cause too much trouble. The light in this composition is coming from the left, so the shadows and highlights are put in accordingly.

The photograph I used as reference for this composition

I have used my imagination for the background colours, choosing tones that complement the delicacy of the flowers.

You will need

Watercolour board
Brushes No. 8 and No. 00
Flat brush: 13mm (½in)
Masking fluid and old brush
Palette for mixing
Watercolour paints: I used cobalt blue; Winsor blue;
  viridian; cadmium yellow; sap green and burnt umber.
Plastic eraser

My outline sketch, with the masking fluid tinted blue for clarity.

Before you begin to paint

Mix the main washes you will need:
A Cobalt blue
B Winsor blue and viridian
C Winsor blue and burnt umber
D Viridian and burnt umber
E Cadmium yellow and sap green

1 Draw an outline sketch (see above) and apply masking fluid to the main flower heads and stems. Mix the main colours you want to use. Wash over the paper with water until the surface is shiny, then repeat the process so that the water sinks in more. Add the Winsor blue and viridian wash using a No. 8 brush.

2 When putting in backgrounds I generally work from light to dark. Add the cadmium yellow and sap green wash...

3 ...and the cobalt blue, working very quickly.

4 Finish adding the washes so that they cover the paper, remembering that they will spread when you tip the board

5 While the paint remains wet, pick up the board and tip the picture slightly so that the colours merge. You can control the direction the colour flows by altering the angle at which you tip the board.

Tip

If your paper begins to dry too much, you can damp it down with plain water from a spray mister rather than touching the paint.

6 Put in some darks beside the flowers to make them stand out, remembering that everything will diffuse on the wet paper, and will also dry lighter.

7 Leave your work to dry thoroughly, or wait until the shine has gone off and use a hair dryer to speed up the process.

8 Reinstate the lines with a 3B pencil, using the initial sketch (see page 84) for guidance if necessary.

9 Using a mix of viridian and burnt umber, paint in negative shapes behind the flowers and leaves.

10 Using a deeper mix of viridian and burnt umber, darken some areas to show up the main flowers and give the painting more depth.

11 Leave your work to dry thoroughly, then rub off the masking fluid with your fingertips.

12 With a flat brush and plain water, gently rub the edges of the coloured areas to soften them.

13 Repeat across the rest of the revealed flowers, neatening any jagged edges.

14 Using the No. 8 brush, mix viridian and cadmium yellow and paint in the tops of the flowers and the stalks, adjusting the intensity of the wash throughout to vary the tones. Remembering where the light is coming from, reserve highlights throughout the painting.

15 Put in detail on the inner petals using lemon yellow, adding a dab of viridian wet-in-wet on top.

16 Using a pale mix of cobalt blue, shade in the petals away from the light and then the petals inside the flowers.

17 With plain water and the point of a fine (No. 00) brush, dampen an area of the background in the shape of a snowdrop.

18 Blot with a pad of absorbent paper to lift out the shape of the flower.

19 Knock the starkness of the lifted-out flower back with a pale wash of cobalt blue. Put in the green top of the flower.

20 Leave the picture to dry thoroughly, then remove the pencil lines with a plastic eraser.

21 Work over the whole painting as necessary, redefining, adding more negative painting in a dark mix of viridian and burnt umber, and generally sharpening up the detail.

The finished painting can be seen on pages 82-83.

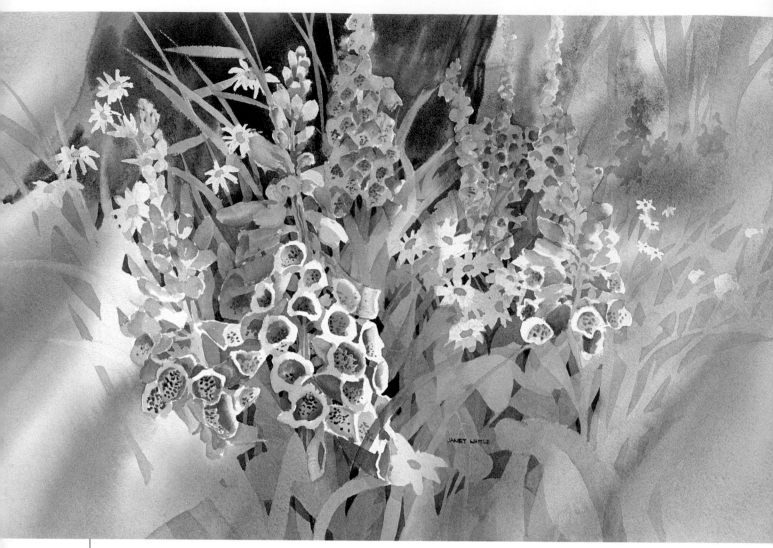

Foxgloves

55 x 38cm (21½ x 15in)

For this letterbox-format composition, I added the background trees to create the impression of the woodland or hedgerows where these flowers often grow, and to show up the main flowers.

Irises

38 x 38cm (15 x 15in)

These flowers were very bright and fresh, so I preserved areas of white to create this effect, putting the whites next to the blues and yellows to keep the whole composition vibrant and alive.

Project
HIMALAYAN POPPY

Watercolour has a reputation for being wishy-washy, but used properly it can be as bright and colourful as any other medium, as this demonstration shows. I have many photographs of this flower as it is one of my favourites, and I used a selection to develop the composition. The negative painting in the background is fairly basic. The petals of the poppies were put in wet-in-wet and the stamens were masked out with dots. I interlocked some of the stamens as, depending on the angle of the flower, they appear more dense in some areas than in others.

The more extremes of tone you can create in a painting, the more vibrant it will be. The green and the blue I used are very similar in tone. This could result in a bland painting, so I compensated by exaggerating the tonal values. I accentuated the brightness of the petals by leaving the white of the paper in places, and towards the centre of the flowers, I deepened the intensity of colour to show up the stamens, making the flowers appear lighter. I placed some of the darks in the background next to the lighter areas of the petals to create depth.

My source photographs

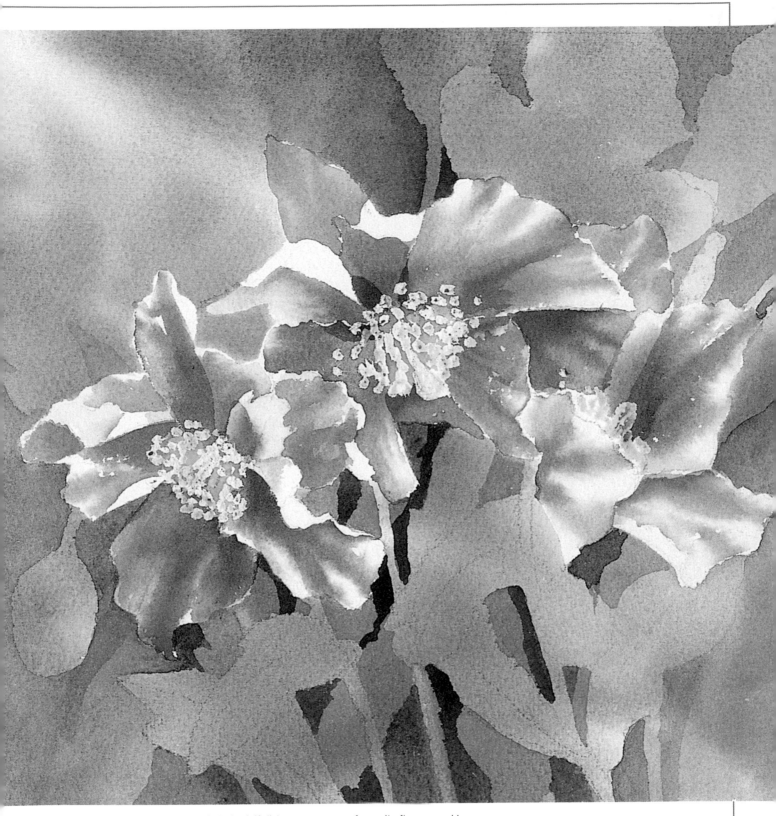

Himalayan poppies (*Meconopsis Betonicifolia*) are among my favourite flowers and I paint them often. I have tried to grow them several times, but sadly they are not happy with the soil in the area where I live. As a result, I take reference photographs of these lovely flowers whenever I get the chance.

You will need

Watercolour paper 300lb (640gsm)
Drawing board and pins
Masking fluid and old brush
Round brush No. 6
Rigger No. 3
Watercolour paint: I used Winsor blue; cobalt blue;
  cadmium yellow; burnt umber; permanent rose; sap
  green; viridian and alizarin crimson

Before you begin to paint

Mix the main washes you will need:
A Viridian and Winsor blue
B Cobalt blue
C Cobalt blue and viridian
D Burnt umber and viridian
E Permanent rose
F Sap green and cadmium yellow

The outline sketch, with masking fluid added to outline the main flowers

1 Pin or stretch your watercolour paper to the drawing board. Mix up the main colours you want to use. Wet the paper up to the masking fluid outline. Using the No. 6 round brush, put in the background colours. Working from light to dark, begin with the yellow mix of sap green and cadmium yellow and follow with the green mix of cobalt blue and viridian and the plain cobalt blue. Let the colours spread right up to the edge of the masking fluid.

2 Tip the paper to merge the washes. Leave your work to dry.

3 Begin to put in the negative painting using the wash of viridian and Winsor blue and following the pencil lines. Let your work dry.

4 Change to the mix of burnt umber and viridian and put in more negative painting, cutting out again within the first negative shape you painted.

5 Rub the masking fluid off the petals, but leave it on the centres. Wet the petals using a No. 6 brush, and put in the cobalt blue wash, followed by a touch of alizarin crimson.

6 Still working wet-in-wet, paint in the rest of the flower petals, dampening each petal and running in the colour, following the tonal values as closely as possible, leaving some hard-edged white areas of dry paper.

7 Deepen the blue on the petals using a mix of Winsor blue with a touch of cobalt blue. Work wet-on-dry and soften the edges with a little water.

8 When your work is dry, remove the masking fluid and paint the stamens in lemon yellow, leaving some white flecks. Deepen the tone with cadmium yellow in the direction away from the light and where the petals would cast a shadow on the stamens. Produce the effect of veining on one or two leaves by putting a slightly deeper wash between the veins so they are light against dark.

The finished painting can be seen on page 93.

Himalayan Poppy

55 x 38cm (21½ x 15in)

A different study of one of my favourite flowers. I worked this painting from photographs taken at Hampton Court Palace, London. It was just after a shower of rain, and they looked absolutely stunning. The delicate blue of the petals and the light shining on them were all the inspiration I needed to paint.

Opposite:

White Cloud

55 x 38cm (21½ x 15in)

Before masking out the shapes of these tree poppies, I put in pale washes of yellows, pinks and blues to take a little of the stark whiteness off the flowers. Negative shapes have been painted in the background wash to cut out the flower shapes.

JANET WHITTLE

This demonstration shows how flowers of very different sizes can be used to complement the focal flowers. The petals of the poppies are painted first in cadmium yellow and, while they are still damp, the red is painted in. The yellow glows through the red, giving a luminous effect. I used the best aspects of several photographs to produce the final composition.

My source photographs

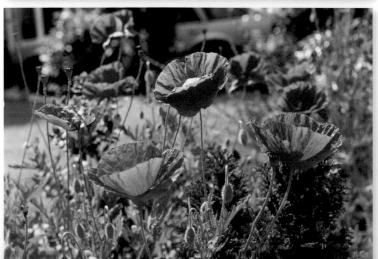

Opposite:
I increased the number of small white daisies in this composition to provide a contrast with the large, brightly coloured poppies.

You will need

Watercolour paper 640gsm (300lb)

Drawing board and pins

Pencils: HB and 3B

Masking fluid and old brush

Round brushes: No. 6 and No. 8

Large soft brush

Watercolour paints: I used cadmium yellow; lemon
   yellow; cobalt blue; viridian; Winsor blue; translucent
   orange; cadmium red and burnt umber.

Before you begin to paint

Mix the main washes you will need:

A Burnt umber and viridian

B Cadmium yellow

C Translucent orange and
   cadmium red

D Lemon yellow and viridian.

E Cobalt blue

F Viridian and Winsor blue

My initial outline sketch, with masking fluid to
outline the main flowers

1 When the masking fluid has dried on
the outline sketch (see above), use a large
round brush, No. 8 or larger, to wet the
paper up to the masking lines, leaving the
flower shapes dry. Load your brush with the
mix of translucent orange and cadmium
red and drop it in behind the flower shapes,
making sure the colour runs up to some of
the masking lines.

2 Continue dropping in background colours, working from light to dark, while the paper is still wet. Begin with cadmium yellow, followed by cobalt blue, the bright green mix and the red mix. Tip the paper to blend the colours slightly. Leave to dry.

3 If you are not happy with the effect, dampen the painting using a brush and drop in more colours. Pick up any excess droplets with a damp brush and leave to dry flat. Draw in the poppies in the background and any additional leaves and stalks you want to include, using a 3B pencil.

4 Paint in the negative shapes behind the background poppies, leaves and stalks using more concentrated mixes of the colours used in the first washes - not too dark, but so that you can see the shapes of the composition.

5   Add some darker negative shapes within the negative shapes you have painted to give the background more depth. Leave your work to dry.

6   Remove the masking fluid by rubbing it gently with your fingertips, then brush away the finings with a large soft brush.

7   Dampen the foreground petals with the No. 8 brush. Painting one petal at a time, put in the cadmium yellow wash, then quickly add the translucent orange and cadmium red wash so that it merges as shown.

8

9

8 To achieve the right effect, paint in the back petals first so they go from dark at the centre to light at the edge ...

9 ...then paint in the petals at the front, leaving a light, soft edge at the top.

10 Complete all the poppies, following the tonal values as closely as possible, as shown here.

10

11 Put in the centres of the daisies, using a wash of cadmium yellow first, then drop in some of the cadmium red and orange wash on the side away from the light.

12 Put in the stamens of the poppies using a dark mix of Winsor blue and burnt umber.

13 The daisies look too stark because with the masking fluid removed they are just white paper...

14 ...so add glazing with a pale wash of cobalt blue to some of them to make them recede into the background slightly and give them some form.

15 Work over the areas of negative painting, sharpening up detail if necessary and adding veins to some of the leaves.

16 Knock back some of the poppies in the background using a pale wash of cobalt blue.

17 Put in the stalks of the poppies that are dark against light using cadmium yellow with a touch of viridian and a No. 6 brush. When dry, remove the pencil lines.

The finished painting can be seen on page 102.

Buff Beauty

55 x 38cm (21½ x 15in)

For this painting, a series of light blushes of colour were put over the paper and allowed to dry, then the flowers were masked on top of the washes. The sunlit areas were also masked to preserve them from the later washes. I mixed different tones of blue and put in the lighter tones first, then dropped in the darker areas wet-in-wet. I painted the flowers with yellows, pinks and orange mixes, then removed the masking and softened the edges. As these areas were now white and a little harsh, I toned some of them down with glazes to push them back.

Opposite:

After the Rain

55 x 38cm (21½ x 15in)

This painting shows how effectively dewdrops can be used in a composition to capture the lovely effects of sunshine after rain. I think it is pure magic, which was why I was inspired to paint these irises. Capturing the moment, and effects which have the power to move you, is what painting is all about.

The background was painted wet-in-wet. I dropped in the colours including the purple I wanted to use on the flowers, so that I could cut out some of the background flowers when the painting was dry to fill out the composition. The petals were painted wet-in-wet. I dampened the petal area first, then dropped in the yellow so it softened off, then, working from the outside edge, I dropped in the purple mix so it too would soften forward, leaving a paler area in the centre of the petal. Timing is all with this technique: if your paper is too wet the colours will bleed too far, and if it is too dry they will not bleed far enough. Practice is essential, but if you find doing the whole thing too daunting, do one colour at a time, wait for it to dry, then wet it again and drop in the other colour.

JANET WHITTLE

Project
SCABIOUS

I have painted the background for this demonstration almost entirely wet-in-wet. This is because scabious leaves are very small and grow mainly at soil level, so I wanted the background to suggest other foliage to add interest and colour to the painting. The centres of these flowers look different when they are newly opened, which makes an interesting feature on some of the blooms.

More interest is added by the way the shades of the flowers vary from white to lavender. Remember if you have good reference material for the flower form you can paint it in different colours as long as they are true to the type of flower. This will add variety to your composition. I have interlocked some of the focal flowers rather than placing them separately like a flower arrangement. I feel this is important because these flowers also grow in the wild and I like to give the impression that they are growing in woodland or hedgerow.

Perspective is also important when you are painting flowers like these. If the flowers tip towards you or away from you, make sure the shape of the centres changes from circular to oval, and that the petals are lengthened or foreshortened accordingly.

You will need

Watercolour paper
Round brush No. 6
Rigger No. 3
3B pencil
Drawing board and pins
Masking fluid and old brush
Watercolour paints: I used cobalt blue; Winsor blue;
    indigo; viridian; lemon yellow; cadmium yellow and
    sap green

Before you begin to paint

Mix the main washes you will need:
A Indigo and Winsor blue
B Cobalt blue
C Viridian and Winsor blue
D Cobalt blue and lemon yellow
E Permanent rose and Winsor blue
F Sap green and lemon yellow

My source photographs

My outline sketch

1 Mask the focal flowers and allow the masking fluid to dry. Using a No. 6 brush, wet the background right up to the masking fluid, and put in the background colours starting with the lightest and working through to the darkest. Tip the board (see page 50) and let the washes blend.

2 Leave these first washes to dry. Note that they will dry quite a lot lighter than they appear when wet. Draw in the background flowers using a 3B pencil.

3 Dampen the paper with plain water. Put in a wash of sap green and lemon yellow using a No. 6 brush, working round the background flowers, then change to a No. 3 rigger and indicate the darker stalks and leaves using a dark mix of indigo and Winsor blue. The shapes can be left abstract, as only an indication rather than detail is required.

4 Let your work dry flat.

5 Put the first colour on the focal flowers using a pale wash of lemon yellow. Paint the centres of the two flowers at the bottom, then drop in some of the sap green mix so that it blends and varies the tone from light to dark.

6 Using the mix of permanent rose and Winsor blue, deepen some of the shadows on the flower heads to give them more depth. Using the dark green mix and the small rigger, paint in between some of the petals next to the centres to indicate separation.

7 Still with the small rigger brush, and with a darker mix of green paint, add detail to the centre of the nearest flower by painting in tiny circles.

8 Darken the circles away from the light on the right hand side and round the edges. This will give the illusion that the middle is raised as the light catches it.

9 Using the permanent rose and Winsor blue mix, deepen some of the shadows on the flower heads to give more depth to the form of the flower, using hard and soft edges.

10 Add circles to the centres of the background flowers, making them fainter because too much detail would bring them too sharply into focus.

11 Glaze over the middles of the foreground flowers to warm them, using a mix of lemon yellow and cadmium yellow. After this, you may need to darken the circles a little on the right.

12 The centres of the two main flowers are slightly different. Paint the hollows using a deeper mix of lemon yellow and cadmium yellow, leaving the edges as white paper. At this stage you should stand back and assess the painting, adjusting the depth of colour where necessary (see inset).

The finished painting can be seen on pages 110–111.

Scabious

37 x 48cm (14½ x 19in)

I dropped soft washes of colour into the background, then allowed them to dry. Negative shapes were added to the background to indicate smaller blooms and one or two stalks. The effect was kept deliberately minimal so the focus of attention would remain on the two main flowers.

Narcissi

38 x 38cm (15 x 15in)

After dropping in washes in the background, I sprinkled salt in the wet paint
to give a textural effect. If you try this, do not dry your work with a hair dryer,
but let it dry naturally. Some colours will give a better result than others, so it
is wise to experiment first.

Project
CLEMATIS

This demonstration brings together many of the techniques found in this book. If you work through it, referring to previous instructions where necessary, it should help to consolidate your skills.

The project is carried out in just four stages: putting in the background; masking the stamens of the flowers (which can be done with a small brush or even a cocktail stick); using negative painting to bring out the detail and putting in the petals wet-in-wet. The colour of the flower has been used in the background to suggest more out-of-focus blooms and buds. Pink is a delicate colour, and to make it more vibrant I have left sunlit areas of white to counterchange the background against it.

My source photographs

These lovely flowers come in an enormous variety of shapes and hues, so you can change the colours to suit yourself.

You will need

Watercolour paper 640gsm (300lb), 55 x 38cm
(21½ x 15in)
3B pencil
Masking fluid and old brush
Brushes: No. 6 round, No. 3, rigger large wash brush
Watercolour paints: permanent rose, cobalt blue,
Winsor blue, viridian, lemon yellow, burnt umber,
magenta, and sap green

Before you begin to paint

Mix the main washes you will need:
A Permanent rose and lemon
    yellow
B Permanent rose
C Sap green
D Cobalt blue
E Viridian and Winsor blue
F Viridian and burnt umber
G Permanent rose and magenta

Use the reference photographs (see page 120) to plan the composition, then
produce an outline sketch (above) using the 3B pencil.

1 Using the large brush, dampen
the paper up to the pencilled
outlines of the flowers and put in
the background, using permanent
rose and lemon yellow; permanent
rose; sap green, and touches of
viridian and Winsor blue. Tip to
merge the colours and leave to dry.

2 Using the No. 6 brush, paint in negative to bring out the leaves and buds using the viridian and burnt umber mix. Leave to dry. Remove the masking fluid at the edges of the flowers, but leave the stamens masked.

3 Wet the white area and paint in the petals wet-in-wet, with the mix of permanent rose. Use a small (No. 3) rigger to drop in a darker mix of permanent rose and magenta. Leave areas of white paper to counterchange against the background.

4 Rub off the masking fluid on the stamen and use a pale wash of lemon yellow to push back some of the white. With the small rigger brush, paint in the tips of the stamens using burnt umber and alizarin crimson (see inset). With the cobalt blue and a small rigger brush, add very fine veins to the centre of some of the petals.

The finished painting can be seen on pages 120–121.

Cosmos

55 x 38cm (21½ x 15in)

Flowers with an overall 'white' effect often have very little white on them when you come to paint them, as this example shows. I saw these growing in France, and the lavender in the background meant that the composition is about blues, pinks and purples. The shadows on the flower petals capture the effect of sunlight. The veining of the flowers has been darkened within the shadow area.

JANET WHITTLE

JANET WHITTLE

Apple Blossoms

46 x 24cm (18 x 9½in)

Towards the back of our garden is an apple orchard. In the spring, it is a riot of blossom which stays for weeks before blowing away quickly in the wind. Beautiful pinks against the spring greens and the darkness of the branches are a tonal gift. I have put soft colours in the background leaving some of the brighter pinks and greens for contrast. We have lived in the same house for many years, and while some things have changed around us, the two remaining apple trees continue to bloom.

INDEX